The

LITTLE BOOK OF

ONE-POT

MEALS

Rufus Cavendish

summersdale

THE LITTLE BOOK OF ONE-POT MEALS

An Hachette UK Company
www.hachette.co.uk

Summersdale Publishers
Part of Octopus Publishing Group Limited
Carmelite House
50 Victoria Embankment
LONDON
EC4Y 0DZ
UK

www.summersdale.com

Printed and bound in Poland

ISBN: 978-1-83799-458-8

This FSC® label means that materials used for the product have been responsibly sourced

MIX
Paper | Supporting
responsible forestry
FSC® C018236

Substantial discounts on bulk quantities of Summersdale books are available to corporations, professional associations and other organizations. For details contact general enquiries: telephone: +44 (0) 1243 771107 or email: enquiries@summersdale.com.

Contents

Introduction

Welcome to *The Little Book of One-Pot Meals*, a veritable cornucopia of deliciously simple yet simply delicious meals that can all be made in your one favourite pot. Whether it's batch cooking for weeknight suppers, bold soups for lunch, impressive one-pot wonders for serving at parties or simplified alternatives to the Sunday roast, in this book we've got you covered.

The best thing about these delicious one-pot centrepieces is that they don't need a plethora of sides and sauces to make them table-worthy; the recipes that follow are truly one-pot meals with all the trimmings, but less of the hassle.

You'll find soups and stews, and roasts and braises, all needing little more than a pan, pot, tin, slow cooker or air fryer to make them a reality on your table. The recipes are easy to follow, and we'll take you step by step through cooking terminology and technique to ensure you're never left high and dry in the middle of a recipe. You'll find tips on menu planning, bulk cooking and how to make the best use of your freezer to ensure you can whip up a one-pot treat with as little fuss and frenzy as possible. We've made sure all of the recipes are easily adaptable for vegetarians and vegans, and you can look at the icon next to each recipe to tell, at a glance, what type of cooking method is required.

So, whether its simplicity, economy or variety that you're after, come on in and try a one-pot meal – you'll never look back.

THE BASICS

Take a moment to read through this chapter and you'll be perfectly prepped for the recipes that follow. These pages cover terminology and techniques, your store cupboard and possible substitutions. The information here will help you to approach the recipes in this book with confidence, as well as any other recipe you might take on one day.

Ten tips for better, quicker cooking

1. Start with a clean kitchen.
2. Don't try to cook while watching the TV or texting on your phone.
3. Put on some music or a podcast that you like.
4. Read the recipe fully before you start cooking.
5. Make sure you have all the ingredients before you start.
6. Prepare all the kit you're going to need.
7. Prep your ingredients before you start cooking, not while you are cooking.
8. Preheat your oven before you start and allow pans to get hot before you use them.
9. Clean up as you go along.
10. Taste as you go and adjust the seasoning at the end.

Essential terminology

Bake: To cook food in an oven, surrounded by dry heat.

Baste: To spoon liquid over food while cooking, for added flavour and to prevent it drying out.

Blanch: To cook briefly in boiling water to seal in flavour and colour; usually used for vegetables or fruit, to prepare for freezing, and to ease skin removal.

Boil: To cook in bubbling, boiling water that has reached 100°C.

Braise: To cook first by browning, then gently simmering in a small amount of liquid over low heat in a covered pan until tender.

Brown (or sear): To cook food over a high heat, usually on top of the stove, until the outer surface achieves a brown colour, sealing in juices and flavour.

Cube: To cut food into small (about 2.5-cm) cubes.

Deglaze: To loosen brown bits from a pan by adding a liquid, then heating while stirring and scraping the pan.

Dice: To cut food into very small (0.5–1-cm) cubes.

Grill: To cook food on a rack under or over direct heat, as on a barbecue or under a salamander grill.

Julienne: To cut an ingredient into long, thin strips, matchstick-like in shape.

Mince: To cut into tiny pieces, almost to a paste and even smaller than when diced, usually with a knife.

Parboil: To partially cook by boiling. Usually done to prepare food for final cooking by another method.

Poach: To cook gently in liquid over very low, simmering heat, only just covering the food.

Reduce: To thicken a liquid and concentrate its flavour by boiling.

Render: To cook fatty meat or poultry – such as bacon or duck – over low heat to melt the fat into the pan.

Roast: To cook food uncovered in an oven at a high temperature.

Sauté or pan-fry: To cook food in a small amount of fat over relatively high heat.

Shred: To cut food into narrow strips with a knife or a grater.

Simmer: To cook in liquid just below the boiling point; small bubbles will blip at the edge of the pan.

Skim: To remove surface foam or fat from a stock, soup or stew.

Stew: To cook a pot of various foods in liquid over low heat.

Stir-fry: To quickly cook small pieces of food over high heat, stirring constantly.

Zest: To grate the outer, coloured part of the peel of citrus fruit.

Equipment

Knives: You need at least one good sharp knife, preferably a chef's knife. If you have one other knife, make it a little "paring" knife, used for smaller precision cutting; and if you want just three essential knives, add a serrated knife that can be used for bread and for some larger fruit and vegetables.

Pots and pans: At a minimum get yourself three pans – one wide shallow pan with a lid, that can double up as a frying and sauté pan; one classic small saucepan; and one large heavy-based or casserole pan large enough to boil pasta in as well as cooking large soups and stews. You can use the casserole in an oven-style air fryer too if it fits. Just remember to adjust recipe temperatures accordingly (see p.17).

Digital scales: A small set of digital scales shouldn't set you back too much and will immediately make you a better, more accurate cook and baker.

Speed peeler: A U-shaped peeler with the blades between the open end is the safest, quickest and best peeler you can own.

Grater: Microplane hand-held graters are all the rage – and have their place – but if you only have one, get a classic box grater with four sides for grating variety.

Hand blender: If you have a blender already you'll find yourself using it a lot in this book. If not – and you don't want to stretch your budget to one – a cheap and cheerful hand blender will be just as good.

Food processor: If you want to take your cooking and baking up a gear, a food processor should be your first big investment. It's not essential, of course, but will make cooking quicker and easier.

Air fryers and slow cookers: The recipes in this book regularly accommodate both air fryers and slow cookers, and where possible suggested temperatures will be given. However, due to the range of settings and options available, it is best to refer to your appliance's manual when converting recipes.

Store-cupboard ingredients

What follows are lists of things you should have in your store cupboard in order to be able to dive into any recipe, any day, safe in the knowledge that you have the spices, tins, dry goods, vinegars, oils and sauces required. These items should always be replaced as they are running out, so stock up on the following ingredients and you'll be set to cook anything and everything you desire.

Oil and vinegar

Oil: You will need an oil – and almost any oil will do. People get excited about extra virgin olive oil – and having one in your cupboard is a good idea for dressings – but it is too strong a flavour for general cooking. For your day-to-day cooking, a mild or relatively flavourless olive or rapeseed oil will do just fine.

Vinegar: For most of your vinegary needs a standard red wine vinegar will do. If you add one other vinegar to your collection it should be apple cider vinegar. Beyond that, a good sherry vinegar and a rice wine vinegar will enable you to cook most dishes from around the world.

Salt, herbs and spices

Salt: Always use fine sea salt for cooking. Buy loose salt and learn to use it with your fingers – this will make you a quicker and better cook.

Black peppercorns: Invest in a grinder and whole peppercorns – they stay fresh longer and you'll be able to taste the pepper in a dish.

Ground spices: Try to have paprika, cumin, cinnamon, ginger, coriander, chilli powder and turmeric. Beyond this, curry powder, garam masala and sumac are very useful.

Whole spices: Try to have cumin, cardamom, nutmeg, cinnamon and fennel seeds.

Herbs: Try keeping dried oregano, thyme and bay leaves. Fresh herbs are nice but you can substitute for a small amount of the dried variety.

Chillies: Always keep dried chilli flakes. Chillies can be specific to certain cuisines, so as you cook more you will pick up things like chipotle, ancho, pul biber and more.

Sauces, condiments and pastes

If you have the following in your store cupboard you'll be able to cook 95 per cent of the dishes in this book and beyond:

- Tahini
- Harissa
- Asian crispy chilli oil
- Fish sauce
- Light soy sauce

- Sriracha
- Tamarind paste
- Chipotle paste
- Dijon mustard
- Mayonnaise
- Tomato purée

Dry goods

Similar to the previous list, so long as you have the following you'll be able to cook almost every dish found in this book:

- Plain flour
- Caster sugar
- Baking powder
- Bicarbonate of soda
- Long-grain rice (such as basmati)
- Short-grain rice (such as arborio)
- A long pasta (linguine is versatile)
- A pasta shape (e.g. rigatoni)

- Lasagne sheets
- Oats
- Split red lentils
- Tinned tomatoes
- Tinned beans (cannellini and black beans are a good place to start)
- Tinned coconut milk
- Frozen peas
- Breadcrumbs

Conversions and measurements

If you don't want to use metric measurements and need some basic conversions handy, refer back to the below:

25 g ≈ 1 oz	15 ml ≈ 0.5 fl oz
60 g ≈ 2 oz	30 ml ≈ 1 fl oz
85 g ≈ 3 oz	75 ml ≈ 2.5 fl oz
115 g ≈ 4 oz	120 ml ≈ 4 fl oz
255 g ≈ 9 oz	270 ml ≈ 9 fl oz

As a rule of thumb, for cooking purposes, Celsius is roughly half the Fahrenheit temperature. Set fan-assisted ovens 25°C (approximately 50°F) lower than others and reduce the time spent cooking by 10 minutes for every hour of cooking time.

To convert an oven recipe for an air fryer, reduce the temperature by 25°C (50°F) and reduce the cooking time by about 20 per cent. Be sure to check that food is piping hot before serving.

Many appliances differ, so check the manufacturer's instructions for further guidance.

QUICK DISHES

We're all busy, we rush around all day, but when the evening comes we have to eat. This chapter covers meals that can be whipped up in under 30 minutes – preparation and cooking included – and tend to contain great-value ingredients that are quick and easy to pull together.

Spanish chickpea stew

 Hob *Serves 4* (Vegan)

This brings together a handful of ingredients to deliver a flavour that packs a punch.

INGREDIENTS

2 tbsp olive oil

2 white onions, peeled and finely chopped

3 garlic cloves, finely grated

2 large red peppers, de-seeded and sliced

200 g cherry tomatoes, whole

1 x 400-g tin chickpeas

2 tbsp sherry vinegar

2 tsp smoked paprika (hot or sweet)

METHOD

Heat the oil and sweat the onions and garlic over a medium heat, stirring occasionally, for 6–8 minutes. Add the peppers and tomatoes and cook for a further 5 minutes until they are just starting to soften, then add the remaining ingredients and bring to a boil. Cover and cook for 10 minutes. Serve with bread or salad and mayonnaise.

Sweet potato chowder

 Hob Serves 4 (Vegetarian)

Traditionally a rich clam soup from New England, this version is lighter and brighter for using sweet potato instead of clams. It hasn't lost the comfort of a classic chowder though, and you can happily add the clams if you prefer.

INGREDIENTS

2 tbsp extra virgin olive oil

1 white onion, finely chopped

1 leek, finely sliced

1 bay leaf

1 tbsp plain flour

300 ml whole milk
 (or oat/soy milk to make vegan)

2 medium potatoes (about 250 g), cubed

1 medium sweet potato, cubed

1 tin sweetcorn

2 tsp sweet smoked paprika

METHOD

Heat the oil and sweat the onion, leek, bay leaf and a good pinch of salt for 6–8 minutes until the vegetables are soft and translucent. Add the flour and stir to make a paste, cook for 2 minutes, then add the milk a little at a time, stirring well between each addition to get a smooth sauce-like consistency. Add the potatoes, simmer for 5 minutes, then add the sweet potato and simmer for a further 10 minutes. Check the potatoes are cooked, add the sweetcorn and the smoked paprika, simmer for another minute or two. Season with plenty of black pepper and a little more salt, if needed, and serve with some crusty bread or salad.

Midweek enchiladas

 Hob   *Serves 2*   (*Vegetarian*)

These super-quick, mouth-watering enchiladas are truly a culinary marvel and make the most of a well-stocked store cupboard. You'll be adding these into your weekly rotation without a doubt.

INGREDIENTS

1 tsp olive oil

1 onion, finely chopped

2 garlic cloves, grated

2 tsp hot smoked paprika

1 tsp ground cumin

400 ml tomato passata

6 small flour tortillas

1 x 400-g tin refried beans

100 g extra-mature cheddar cheese (or any hard cheese of your choice), grated

200 g sour cream

METHOD

Heat an ovenproof casserole pan or skillet over a medium heat and warm the oil. Add the onion and garlic, and cook for 6–8 minutes until soft and brown at the edges. Add the paprika, cumin and a good pinch of salt. Cook for 1 minute more, then add the passata and bring back to a simmer.

Meanwhile, preheat your grill to its hottest setting. Next, add 2 tbsp refried beans to the middle of each tortilla, as well as 1 tbsp grated cheese. Roll into fat cigars and place to one side, seam-side down. Once the tortillas are rolled, remove the sauce from the heat. Place the tortillas into the liquid, pressing to slightly submerge but not sink entirely. Spread the sour cream over the top followed by the remaining grated cheese. Place under the grill and cook for 5–7 minutes, removing once the cheese is bubbly and brown. Allow to cool before serving.

Risi e bisi

 Hob   *Serves 2*   (*Vegetarian*)

This is a simple way to achieve something close to a risotto.

INGREDIENTS

2 tbsp olive oil

2 white onions, finely chopped

2 garlic cloves, grated

200 g risotto rice

1 litre hot vegetable stock

400 g frozen peas, defrosted

2 tbsp grated vegetarian hard cheese

METHOD

Heat the oil in a heavy-based or casserole pan over a medium heat. Add onions and cook gently for 6–8 minutes until softening but not browned. Add garlic, cook for 1 minute, then add rice and a pinch of salt and cook for another couple of minutes. Add stock and peas and simmer for 10–15 minutes, or until the rice is just cooked. Then add vegetarian hard cheese and season to taste with salt and pepper.

Prawn and tomato orzo

▤ *Oven*   ⊕ *Air Fryer*   *Serves 4*

Simply toss everything into an ovenproof dish, and this elegant meal will transport you to somewhere sun-kissed and far away.

INGREDIENTS

1 red onion, chopped

2 garlic cloves, grated

1 red chilli, deseeded and chopped

1 x 400-g tin chopped tomatoes

400 g orzo pasta

800 ml vegetable stock

400 g frozen king prawns

25 g basil, roughly torn

METHOD

Preheat your oven to 200°C (air fryer; 175°C). In a medium-sized ovenproof dish, combine all ingredients apart from the prawns and basil. Season with salt and mix well. Spread the prawns over the top, pressing slightly so they are partly submerged. Bake, uncovered, for 20–25 minutes (air fryer; 15–20 minutes). The orzo should soak up the liquid; the prawns should be bright pink and catching at the edges. Tear the basil over the top to serve.

Broccoli orecchiette

 Hob　　　　　*Serves 2*　　(*Vegan*)

Love pasta but hate using multiple pans for a simple dish?
Bung this all in one pan and whistle while it cooks.

INGREDIENTS

250 g orecchiette pasta

300 g Tenderstem broccoli, chopped into 3-cm pieces

8 cherry tomatoes, halved

2 garlic cloves, finely sliced

4 spring onions, finely chopped

1 lemon, zested and juiced

2 tbsp olive oil

1 vegetable stock cube, crumbled

½ tsp dried chilli flakes

METHOD

Place all the ingredients into a large saucepan along with 800 ml water and 1 tsp salt. Bring to the boil, then reduce the heat to low and cook for 6–8 minutes, stirring occasionally, until the pasta is cooked and the broccoli and tomato have broken down to create a delicious sauce. Season to taste and serve.

Crispy chilli mushroom udon

 Hob   *Serves 2*   (*Vegan*)

This fiery udon dish packs a punch way above its complexity.

INGREDIENTS

2 tbsp olive oil

300 g chestnut mushrooms, finely chopped

8 spring onions, finely chopped

2 tbsp light soy sauce

1 tbsp smooth peanut butter

2 tbsp crispy chilli oil

400 g udon noodles

METHOD

Heat oil in a large frying pan over a medium heat. Add mushrooms and fry for 5-6 minutes until they start to colour. Add two-thirds of the spring onions, soy sauce, peanut butter, crispy chilli oil and 100 ml water. Bring to a simmer, add the udon and mix. Cook for 3-5 minutes, until the udon are cooked. Serve with remaining spring onions and extra chilli oil.

Creamy mushroom tortellini

 Hob    *Air Fryer*   *Serves 4*   (Vegetarian)

A genius way to bring together everyday store-cupboard staples to create a rich and unctuous dish that feels as if you've spent all day in the kitchen.

INGREDIENTS

1 x 400-g tin cream of mushroom soup
125 ml white wine
125 ml double cream
¼ tsp freshly ground black pepper
1 lemon, zested and juiced
500 g fresh or frozen tortellini, thawed
100 g breadcrumbs
50 g freshly grated vegetarian hard cheese

METHOD

Preheat your grill to its hottest setting. Place a casserole pan over a medium heat (air fryer; 180°C) and add the soup, white wine, cream and a pinch of salt to the pan. Bring to a simmer (air fryer; 3-4 minutes), then remove from the heat and add the black pepper, lemon juice and tortellini, stirring and pressing down so that they are completely covered by the sauce. Top with the breadcrumbs, grated vegetarian hard cheese and lemon zest, and place under the hot grill (or in the air fryer on its hottest grill setting) for 5-7 minutes until the sauce is bubbling and you have a golden-brown crust. Allow to cool slightly before serving.

Quick mushroom and coconut noodles

 Hob *Serves 2* (*Vegan*)

Traditionally ramen is a broth that should be cooked for eight or more hours, but this is ready in under 30 minutes and is vegan. You can't say fairer than that.

INGREDIENTS

1 tbsp oil

4 spring onions, finely sliced

1 red chilli, finely sliced

3 garlic cloves, grated

1 tsp fresh ginger, grated

150 g chestnut mushrooms, finely sliced

2 tbsp miso paste

1 tbsp light soy sauce

500 ml vegetable stock

250 ml coconut milk

400 g udon noodles

1 lime, juiced

25 g coriander, leaves picked

METHOD

Place a large pan over a medium heat and add the oil. Once hot, fry the spring onions, chilli, garlic and ginger for 2 minutes, then add the mushrooms and cook for a few minutes. Mix in the miso paste and soy sauce, add the stock and coconut milk, bring to a boil and allow to simmer for 5-6 minutes. Add the noodles and cook for a further 3 minutes. Finally, season with lime juice and top with coriander.

Chicken and chorizo paella

 Hob   *Serves 4*

Knocking up a proper paella takes time, and it is worth it, but sometimes we want a Spanish treat in a matter of minutes – so thank goodness for precooked rice.

INGREDIENTS

1 tbsp oil

1 white onion, finely diced

2 garlic cloves, grated

150 g chorizo, cut into 2-cm slices

250 g precooked chicken

300 g tomatoes, roughly chopped

2 x 250-g pouches precooked rice

10 g flat leaf parsley, roughly chopped

Lemon wedge, to serve (optional)

METHOD

Heat the oil in a wide-based saucepan over a medium heat. Add onion, garlic and a pinch of salt and fry for 4–5 minutes before adding the chorizo and cooking for a further 4–5 minutes. Add tomato, chicken and rice, combine well, cover and cook for a final 5 minutes. Leave to cool slightly, then scatter with parsley and a squeeze of lemon to serve.

Kale and lentil stew

🍲 *Hob*   *Serves 4*   (Vegan)

Hearty and warming, this is for when you want to feel virtuous, but also need a hug from your belly. You'll be full and nourished, and very happy indeed.

INGREDIENTS

2 tbsp olive oil

1 white onion, finely chopped

2 sticks celery, finely chopped

2 garlic cloves, grated

1 red chilli, finely sliced, seeds and all

1 x 400-g tin cooked lentils

200 g kale or cavolo nero, roughly chopped

METHOD

Heat the oil in a large saucepan or casserole pan. Add the onion, celery, garlic, chilli and a good pinch of salt, and sweat for 6–8 minutes until softening. Add the lentils, juice and all, then fill the tin with water and add this too, bringing everything to a simmer. Add the kale and cook for a further 5 minutes before seasoning and serving.

Spring dhal

 Hob   *Serves 4*   (*Vegan*)

A great way to use up any glut of spring vegetables, this feels fresh and bright while also being warm enough to comfort you as the temperature drops on a nice spring evening.

INGREDIENTS

2 tbsp oil

1 white onion, finely chopped

3 tsp fresh ginger, grated

3 tsp ground cumin

3 tsp ground coriander

½ tsp ground turmeric

¼ tsp chilli powder

400 g spring veg, chopped into 2-cm pieces (courgettes, asparagus, broccoli, spinach, peas and broad beans work well)

200 g split red lentils, washed

25 g coriander, leaves picked

METHOD

Heat the oil in a large, covered saucepan over a medium heat. Add the onion and a good pinch of salt and cook for 6–8 minutes until soft. Add the ginger and cook for another minute or so, then add the spices and cook for a further 30 seconds. Add your chopped veg and lentils and 1 litre of boiling water. Bring to a simmer and cook for 15 minutes. Add more salt or spices as necessary. Scatter coriander over to serve.

Prawn laksa

                                    Serves 2

With all the time in the world you could make your own
laksa paste and feel like a master chef in your own kitchen,
but this is a weeknight and we want something soupy,
spicy, fresh and delicious in under an hour, so we're using
a shop-bought paste. Otherwise, you could be in Malaysia
eating this on a street corner and sweating buckets.

INGREDIENTS

1 tbsp oil

1 tbsp laksa paste

1 x 400-ml tin coconut
milk

200 g frozen king
prawns

1 head pak choi,
cut into quarters
lengthways

4 spring onions, finely
sliced

200 g vermicelli rice
noodles

1 lime, halved

1 tbsp light soy sauce

25 g coriander, leaves
picked

METHOD

Heat the oil in a large saucepan or casserole pan and add the laksa paste, frying it for a minute or so to release its flavours. Add the coconut milk, then fill the tin with water and add this too. Bring to the boil then simmer for 10 minutes to intensify the flavour. Add the prawns, pak choi, spring onions, and noodles, and cook for a further 4 minutes, or until the prawns are bright pink and cooked through, and the noodles are nicely cooked. Season with the juice of half a lime and soy sauce. Serve with coriander and a wedge of lime.

Szechuan aubergine noodles

 Hob   *Serves 2*   (*Vegetarian*)

Aubergines are much maligned as mushy and tasteless, but here, with the help of some Szechuan peppercorns and careful frying by you, they become rich and meaty little morsels amongst the long and luscious noodles.

INGREDIENTS

3 tbsp oil

1 aubergine, cut into 2-cm cubes

2 sticks celery, finely chopped

1 tsp cumin seeds

1 tsp Szechuan peppercorns

2 tbsp crispy chilli oil

1 tbsp rice wine vinegar

2 tbsp light soy sauce

200 g egg noodles (or wholewheat noodles to make the dish vegan), cooked as per the packet instructions

5 g mint, leaves picked and roughly chopped

METHOD

Heat the oil in a large frying pan or wok over a medium-high heat. Add the aubergine in a single layer (frying in batches if your pan isn't large enough) and cook for 4–5 minutes, tossing occasionally, until softened and browned all over. Add the celery, cumin seeds and Szechuan peppercorns, and cook for a further 2–3 minutes. Add the crispy chilli oil, vinegar and soy sauce, and bring to a simmer. Add the cooked noodles and toss to coat. Add more soy or vinegar if needed. Finally, toss through the mint before serving.

Egg-fried chicken and mushroom rice

 Hob   *Serves 2*

If you're someone who likes to keep leftovers in the fridge, then you're the perfect candidate for an egg-fried rice. Any scraps of pork, chicken or beef could find their way into this dish. As could most vegetables, cooked or raw, that you might have lying about. Here we're using peas, mushrooms and pieces of cooked chicken, but substitute these to your heart's content.

INGREDIENTS

2 tbsp oil

100 g chicken, cooked or raw, cut into bite-sized pieces.

100 g mushrooms, chopped

100 g frozen peas

250 g leftover rice (or precooked/ microwave rice)

2 eggs, beaten

1 tbsp light soy sauce

2 spring onions, finely sliced

METHOD

Heat the oil in a large frying pan or wok over a high heat. Add the chicken pieces and chopped mushrooms and fry for 2–3 minutes until starting to colour (if using raw chicken, cook this for 3 minutes or so before adding the mushrooms). Add the peas and cooked rice, frying for 2–3 minutes until piping hot. Push everything to one side of the pan and add the eggs. Let this set a little before breaking it up and stirring through the rest of the rice. Add the soy sauce and spring onions, and stir to combine and coat everything. Serve while still piping hot, perhaps with a chilli sauce for some extra heat.

Crispy chilli tofu and Tenderstem broccoli

 Hob   *Serves 2*   (*Vegan*)

These crispy tofu nuggets, coated in chilli sauce and combined with burned broccoli, are the naughty midweek treat you never knew you needed.

INGREDIENTS

3 tbsp oil

250 g firm tofu, cut into 3-cm cubes

1 tbsp cornflour

150 g Tenderstem broccoli, halved lengthways

2 tbsp sriracha

2 tbsp rice wine vinegar

3 tbsp light soy sauce

2 spring onions, finely chopped

25 g coriander, leaves picked

1 lime, halved

METHOD

Toss the cubes of tofu in the cornflour and season with a pinch of salt. Heat 1 tbsp oil in a large frying pan over a high heat. Add the broccoli, cooking for 2-3 minutes per side until almost burned. Remove from the pan and leave to one side. Add the remaining oil to the pan. Once hot, add the dusted tofu, browning all over. Once golden brown, add the sriracha, vinegar and soy sauce, and simmer for a few minutes until it is sticky and coating the crispy tofu. Add the broccoli back to the pan along with the spring onions and coriander. This can be plated alongside rice or noodles, but doesn't need to be. Serve with a wedge of lime.

Provençal tomato tart

🍳 *Oven*   🍲 *Air Fryer*   *Serves 4*   (*Vegetarian*)

This tart is perfect for a summery lunch or a light supper.

INGREDIENTS

- 1 pack ready-rolled puff pastry
- 1 tbsp olive oil
- 2 tbsp crème fraîche
- ½ lemon, zested
- 4 vine tomatoes, sliced
- 1 garlic clove, finely sliced
- 10 g thyme, leaves picked and chopped
- Small handful basil, torn

METHOD

Preheat the oven to 250°C (air fryer; 225°C). Unfurl pastry on a baking tray and score a 2.5-cm border. Brush the edges with some of the olive oil. Inside the border, spread crème fraîche in an even layer and add lemon zest. Lay tomatoes on top and scatter over garlic, thyme and a good pinch of salt. Drizzle with remaining oil and bake for 15–20 minutes (air fryer; 10–15 minutes). Once the pastry is golden brown, scatter over the torn basil and serve.

Fridge-raid tortilla

     Serves 2   (Vegetarian)

With a few eggs and a fridge full of odds and ends, you're little more than a few minutes away from a perfect Spanish tortilla.

INGREDIENTS

2 tbsp olive oil

1 white onion, finely sliced

1 x 25-g pack ready salted crisps

100 g leftover veg, roughly chopped

6 medium eggs, beaten

50 g feta, crumbled

METHOD

Heat oil in a frying pan over a medium heat. Add onion and a pinch of salt. Cook for 8–10 minutes, until soft. Add crisps and chopped veg and toss together. Then add eggs and stir. Scatter the feta and cook for 4–5 minutes until the egg is completely set. Use a plate to flip the tortilla out of the pan, then slide it back in to cook for 1 minute on the other side. Serve in wedges.

Spring/summer pad thai

 Hob   *Serves 2*   (Vegetarian)

A good pad thai is an undeniable joy. One that is ready in less than 30 minutes should be celebrated as a miracle.

INGREDIENTS

200 g flat rice noodles

1 tbsp oil

1 red chilli, finely sliced, seeds and all

2 garlic cloves, grated

4 spring onions, finely sliced

2 tbsp tamarind paste

2 tbsp light soy sauce

1 tbsp caster sugar

2 eggs, beaten

1 bunch asparagus, finely sliced

8–10 green beans, chopped into 5-mm pieces

1 lime; ½ juiced, ½ cut into wedges

50 g salted peanuts, finely chopped (or bashed)

METHOD

Start by soaking the noodles in boiling water for 10 minutes. Meanwhile, heat a large frying pan or wok over a medium heat. Add the oil, followed by the chilli and garlic, and cook for a minute, or until the garlic just starts to brown. Add the spring onions, followed by the tamarind, soy sauce and sugar. Toss this about for a minute, add the beaten egg and stir while it cooks, much like scrambled egg. Drain the noodles and add these to the pan, stirring everything together so that the spiced egg mixture coats the noodles. Finally, add the chopped raw spring veg along with the lime juice and chopped/bashed peanuts and toss a few more times, frying for a further 2-3 minutes. Check the seasoning, adding more lime juice or soy sauce depending on your preference. Serve with a wedge of lime.

French seafood soup

🍲 *Hob*   *Serves 4*

This meal was traditionally knocked up in French harbours to enjoy the best of the day's catch.

INGREDIENTS

2 tbsp olive oil
1 leek, finely sliced
2 garlic cloves, sliced
8 strands of saffron
150 ml rosé wine
600 g frozen seafood selection, which

should contain prawns, mussels, squid and white fish
4 tbsp crème fraîche
4 sprigs tarragon, leaves removed and roughly chopped

METHOD

Heat the oil in a large saucepan over a medium heat. Add the leek, garlic and saffron and sweat for 6–8 minutes, stirring occasionally. Add the wine and simmer for a few minutes. Add the frozen seafood and 500 ml of boiling water and simmer for 5 minutes until the seafood is cooked through. Finally, mix through the crème fraîche and tarragon and serve with some crusty bread.

Warming chickpea curry

 Hob   *Serves 2*   (*Vegan*)

This vibrant curry needs nothing more to make it a main meal, but you can add a warm naan bread if you desire.

INGREDIENTS

2 tbsp coconut oil

1 onion, chopped

2 garlic cloves, grated

2 green chillies, finely chopped

1 tbsp curry powder

1 sweet potato, chopped into 2-cm cubes

1 x 400-g tin chickpeas

1 x 400-ml tin coconut milk

2 handfuls baby spinach

1 lime, juiced

METHOD

Heat the oil in a wide, shallow saucepan. Add onion, garlic, chilli and a pinch of salt. Cook until soft, then add curry powder and sweet potato, cooking for 2 minutes. Add chickpeas, their juice and the coconut milk. Bring to the boil, then simmer for 10 minutes. Add spinach and lime juice, stirring to help it wilt. Check the seasoning and serve.

Lightning pho

 Hob   *Serves 2*

Much like Japanese ramen, this Vietnamese broth would traditionally take hours to bubble away before it's ready for the table. Here, with a few shortcuts, we can have something very tasty that does the job in well under 30 minutes – lightning fast as the name suggests.

INGREDIENTS

600 ml chicken or vegetable stock

1 garlic clove, grated

3 tsp fresh ginger, grated

1 cinnamon stick

2 star anise

1 tsp fennel seeds

1 red chilli, halved lengthways

2 tbsp light soy sauce

2 tsp fish sauce (optional, leave out to make vegan)

50 g rice vermicelli noodles

120 g leftover/precooked pork, chicken or beef (or vegetables/ pre-prepared tofu)

1 lime, halved

25 g mint and/or coriander, leaves picked

METHOD

Bring the stock to the boil in a large saucepan. Add the garlic, ginger, cinnamon, star anise, fennel seeds, halved chilli, soy and fish sauce, and simmer gently for 10 minutes. Add the noodles and prepare in the broth as per the packet instructions, but likely for 3–5 minutes until cooked. Taste the broth and adjust the seasoning with more soy sauce as needed.

Finally, spoon your broth into bowls, dividing the noodles evenly between them, and then top each pho with your chosen combination of sliced meat, veg or tofu, a good squeeze of lime and plenty of the mint or coriander leaves.

WEEKNIGHT STAPLES

Weeknight suppers can sometimes feel like a chore and it might be tempting to order in or opt for a ready meal, but having a stock of quick and simple recipes to rustle up in under an hour will have you feeling smug and virtuous while eating well.

Tuscan roasted sausages

🗲 *Oven*   🍳 *Air Fryer*   *Serves 4*

Roasting a tray of ingredients has never been so rewarding.

INGREDIENTS

1 head fennel, cut into eighths

400 g new potatoes, quartered

4 garlic cloves, halved

1 lemon, cut into eighths

150 g cherry tomatoes, halved

8 good pork sausages (or vegan/vegetarian sausages if you prefer)

2 tbsp olive oil

100 g rocket

METHOD

Preheat oven to 200°C (air fryer; 175°C). Place everything except the rocket into a large roasting tray with a good pinch of salt. Mix well, then arrange everything into a single layer with the sausages sitting slightly on top. Bake for 30 minutes (air fryer; 25 minutes) until the sausages are cooked through, and the fennel and potatoes are soft and slightly browned. Add the rocket to serve.

Greek chicken and orzo

 Hob   *Serves 4*

Versatile and super simple, serve straight from the oven for a warming winter stew or at room temperature in warmer months for a surprisingly light al fresco treat.

INGREDIENTS

2 tbsp olive oil

8 chicken thighs

1 red onion, diced

2 garlic cloves, minced

1 tsp salt

200 g orzo pasta

250 ml chicken or vegetable stock

2 x 400-g tins chopped tomatoes

1 tbsp dried oregano

12 black olives, pitted and halved

100 g feta, cubed

METHOD

In a casserole or shallow pan with a lid, warm the oil over a medium heat. Add the chicken thighs skin-side down and cook for 6–8 minutes or until the skin is golden brown and the fat has been rendered into the pan. Remove the chicken to a plate and add the onion, garlic and salt to the pan, stirring in the hot oil and rendered fat for a few minutes. Add the orzo, stock and tomatoes and bring to a simmer. Add the chicken back to the pan along with the oregano and olives, place the lid on the pan and simmer for 12–15 minutes or until all the orzo is cooked through. Remove the lid, crumble the feta over the top and serve.

Minestrone

 Hob Serves 4 (Vegan)

This luxurious Italian soup is far more than the sum of its parts. Little more than good vegetables and beans are turned into a rich soup that can hold its own as a lunchtime staple or a warming evening meal.

INGREDIENTS

4 tbsp olive oil

2 onions, finely sliced

1 tsp salt

8 leaves of cavolo nero or kale, leaves removed from the stalks and shredded

2 courgettes, cubed

2 sticks celery, diced

2 carrots, diced

2 potatoes, diced

2 x 400-g tins plum tomatoes, rinsed and juice discarded

1 x 400-g tin cannellini beans, juice and all

1 litre veg stock (or water)

100 g pasta, could be broken spaghetti/vermicelli or even penne/rigatoni that has been smashed into smaller pieces

METHOD

Heat the oil in a large saucepan with a lid over medium heat. Add the onions and salt and cook for 5-6 minutes, stirring regularly, until the onions are soft but not browned. Add the cavolo nero, courgettes, celery, potatoes and tomatoes and cook for 8-10 minutes, stirring occasionally. Add the beans, along with the juice from the tin and the stock, plus enough water to cover everything in the pan. Simmer for 45 minutes before adding the pasta and cooking for a further 8-10 minutes or until the pasta is cooked. Top each portion with a good splash of olive oil.

Baked halloumi ratatouille

 Oven　　 *Air Fryer*　　　*Serves 4*　　(Vegetarian)

A coming together of two wonderful things – the pleasing chew of the halloumi is a wonderful contrast to the soft rich ratatouille. In spring, summer, autumn or winter, this is a wonderful meal as it is, or served with crusty bread and butter.

INGREDIENTS

4 tbsp olive oil

2 red onions, finely sliced

2 garlic cloves, finely sliced

400 g large tomatoes, roughly chopped

25 g basil leaves

2 aubergines, sliced into rounds 5 mm thick

2 courgettes, sliced into rounds 5 mm thick

400 g halloumi, cut into slices 5 mm thick

METHOD

Preheat the oven to 250°C (air fryer; 225°C). In a shallow saucepan or casserole pan, briefly fry the onions and garlic in 2 tbsp olive oil over a medium heat. Add the tomatoes and half the basil and cook for 5-6 minutes until the tomatoes are starting to break down and turn saucy. Remove from the heat and carefully arrange slices of aubergine, courgette and halloumi in an alternating pattern around the pan so that by the end you have concentric circles of veg and cheese with the tomato sauce underneath. Drizzle with the remaining oil and place in the hot oven to bake for 25-30 minutes (air fryer; 20-25 minutes), or until all the veg is soft and golden brown on top. Allow to cool slightly before tearing over the remaining basil and serving.

Spanish squid and potato stew

 Hob   *Serves 4*

We don't often reach for squid when we think of a weeknight supper, but you can easily buy good frozen squid – and it's more exciting than chicken thighs, isn't it?

INGREDIENTS

2 tbsp olive oil

1 red onion, roughly chopped

2 garlic cloves, grated

2 tsp fennel seeds

1 tbsp sweet smoked paprika

2 x 400-g tins chopped tomatoes

800 g frozen squid tubes

500 g waxy potatoes, peeled and cut into 3-cm cubes

2 tbsp sherry or cider vinegar

METHOD

Heat the oil in a large, shallow or casserole pan. Add the onion, garlic and a good pinch of salt and sweat for 8-10 minutes over a medium-low heat. Add the fennel seeds and paprika, cook for 1 minute, then add the tinned tomatoes and squid. Bring this to the boil and leave to simmer for 25 minutes. Add the potato and cook for a further 15 minutes before seasoning with the vinegar and a little more salt if needed. Serve as it is, or with some bread to mop up all the tasty sauce.

Chinese-style baked fish

 Oven   *Air Fryer*   *Serves 2*

For this recipe, you need to know how to make an envelope out of baking paper. Beyond that, these little parcels of fragrant fish and vegetables take no time to make.

INGREDIENTS

1 head fennel, cut into eighths

2 heads pak choi, halved

125 g shiitake mushrooms, halved

2 x 200-g fillets of fish (cod, halibut, salmon or sea bass would work well)

3 tsp fresh ginger, finely sliced

2 garlic cloves, finely sliced

1 red chilli, finely sliced, seeds and all

2 tbsp light soy sauce

2 tbsp rice wine vinegar

METHOD

Preheat the oven to 200°C (air fryer; 175°C). Take two sheets of baking paper about 40 x 40 cm in size. Working on the left half of each sheet, replicating the process for both, lay half the fennel, half a pak choi and half the mushrooms in a pile. Onto this place one piece of fish. Top the fish with slices of ginger, garlic and chilli. In a bowl combine the soy sauce and vinegar. Fold the baking paper in half over the fish and vegetables so that you have the makings of a parcel. Working on the short edges first, neatly fold the edges over on themselves three of four times. Into the open front of the envelope, spoon half the sauce before folding this side over a few times too, to seal. Carefully place these parcels onto a baking sheet and into the hot oven for 15 minutes (air fryer; 10-12 minutes). To serve, simply tear or cut open the parcels and tuck in.

Lamb keema pav

 Hob   *Serves 4*

In India, a pav tends to be a curry served in a bun or dinner roll, and this is how I recommend eating it. You could also serve it with a naan or rice, but that is somehow less fun.

INGREDIENTS

2 tbsp oil
2 onions, finely chopped
4 garlic cloves, grated
4 tsp fresh ginger, grated
2 tbsp garam masala
1 tbsp chilli powder (optional)
600 g lamb mince
1 x 400-g tin chopped tomatoes
250 g frozen peas
2 medium potatoes, cut into 1-cm cubes

METHOD

Heat the oil in a pan over a medium heat. Add the onions, garlic, ginger and a good pinch of salt and cook for 6-8 minutes. Add the spices and the lamb mince and continue to cook for 4-6 minutes more until the lamb mince is browning. Add the tinned tomatoes, peas and potatoes, then use the tomato tin to add 800 ml of water (i.e. fill it twice) and bring to a simmer. Cook for 15 minutes, or until the potatoes are cooked. For the authentic experience, fill a toasted bread roll or two with the mince and eat. Alternatively, serve alongside rice or naan.

Boston baked sausages

 Hob   *Serves 4*

Hearty and (relatively) healthy, this is the perfect winter warmer.

INGREDIENTS

2 tbsp extra virgin olive oil

8 pork sausages

1 small white onion, diced

2 garlic cloves, grated

1 x 400-g tin cannellini beans

1 tbsp Dijon mustard

2 tbsp dark brown sugar

2 tbsp tomato ketchup

200 ml chicken stock

METHOD

Add the oil to a heavy-bottomed or casserole pan over a medium heat. Fry the sausages until browned, about 2–3 minutes per side. Add onion, garlic and a pinch of salt and cook for 6–8 minutes. Once softened, add the beans and their liquid and scrape up any residue from the pan. Add all remaining ingredients, cover, reduce to a simmer and cook for 30 minutes. Serve with crusty bread or a salad.

Roasted cauli couscous

🔲 *Oven*   🍽 *Air Fryer*   *Serves 4*   (*Vegan*)

This combination of roasted cauliflower with Middle Eastern spices is hard to resist.

INGREDIENTS

2 tbsp olive oil

1 large cauliflower, florets separated

2 tbsp ground cumin

1 tbsp ground coriander

2 tsp dried chilli flakes

150 g couscous

10 g mint, leaves picked and chopped

10 g coriander, leaves picked and chopped

1 lemon, juiced

METHOD

Preheat oven to 200°C (air fryer; 175°C). Add oil, cauliflower, cumin, coriander, chilli and a pinch of salt to a roasting tin and mix well. Roast for 30 minutes (air fryer; 25 minutes). Remove from oven. Scatter couscous around the florets then pour in enough boiling water to just cover the couscous. Seal with tinfoil, leave for 10 minutes, then add the herbs and lemon juice. Mix well and serve.

Harissa lamb, freekeh and Tenderstem broccoli

 Hob   *Serves 4*

It's hard to categorize this, but a Middle Eastern soupy stew is about what we're dealing with here.

INGREDIENTS

2 tbsp oil

1 red onion, chopped

2 sticks celery, chopped

4 garlic cloves

300 g lamb leg, diced

2 tsp ground cumin

100 g freekeh (or bulgur wheat if freekeh is hard to find)

1.5 litres vegetable stock

150 g Tenderstem broccoli, roughly chopped

1 tbsp harissa paste

10 g mint, leaves picked

METHOD

Heat the oil in a large pan over a medium heat and sweat the onion, celery and garlic for 6-8 minutes, stirring occasionally. Add the lamb, cumin and a good pinch of salt and cook for a further 6-8 minutes until the lamb is browned all over. Add the freekeh and stir this through the lamby onions. Add the vegetable stock and bring to a boil. Reduce to a simmer and leave to cook for 30 minutes before adding the broccoli and harissa paste and cooking for a final 4 minutes. Check the seasoning, adding more salt or harissa if needed, before adding the mint and serving in big bowls, perhaps with a pitta bread or similar for dunking.

Kitchari

 Hob   *Serves 4*   (*Vegan*)

A mix of spices, rices and lentils, this is said to be the inspiration for kedgeree. No smoked fish or hard-boiled eggs here though, just perfectly spiced rice.

INGREDIENTS

2 tbsp oil

2 dried chillies

1 tsp fennel seeds

1 tsp cumin seeds

1 onion, sliced

4 garlic cloves, grated

3 tsp fresh ginger, grated

120 g basmati rice

120 g split red lentils

50 g green beans, cut into 1-cm pieces

1 tsp turmeric

25 g coriander, leaves picked

1 lime, juiced

METHOD

Heat the oil in a wide and shallow covered saucepan over a medium heat. Add the chillies, fennel seeds and cumin seeds, sizzling for a few seconds, before adding the onion, garlic, ginger and a good pinch of salt. Cook for 6–8 minutes, stirring occasionally, until the onion is soft and starting to colour. Add the rice and lentils and stir to coat everything with the spiced onions. Add the green beans and the turmeric and pour in 750 ml of boiling water. Bring to the boil, reduce the heat to low, place a lid on the pan and cook for 20 minutes. Check after 10 and 15 minutes and add a splash more boiling water if the mix is looking dry. Make sure the rice and lentils are cooked, then leave to one side with the lid on for 5 minutes. Sprinkle with coriander and stir through the juice of one lime, then serve.

Sweet potato and aubergine curry with dumplings

 Hob   *Slow Cooker*   *Serves 4*   (Vegan)

This rich West Indian coconut curry is a belly-warming meal that will put a smile on your face even on the greyest days.

INGREDIENTS

4 tbsp oil

1 onion, chopped

2 carrots, chopped

4 garlic cloves, halved

5 sprigs thyme

150 g plain flour

4 tsp fresh ginger, grated

2 tbsp curry powder

1 Scotch bonnet chilli (or a couple of red chillies if you can't find it)

2 aubergines, cut into 2-cm cubes

1 sweet potato, cut into 2-cm cubes

2 x 400-ml tins coconut milk

2 limes, juiced

METHOD

Heat 2 tbsp oil in a large, covered saucepan or casserole pan over a medium heat. Add the onion, carrots, garlic, thyme and a good pinch of salt and cook for 8–10 minutes. While this is cooking, add the flour to a bowl with the remaining 2 tbsp oil and 100 ml warm water and mix to a dough. Leave to one side. Once the onions are soft, add the ginger, curry powder and Scotch bonnet and cook for a further 2 minutes. Add the aubergines and sweet potato, stirring to coat in the spiced onion mix, then pour in the coconut milk and lime juice and bring to a simmer. Now take the dough and portion eight little dumplings, drop these into the stew so they sit on the surface. Cook for 15–20 minutes until the sweet potato is tender and the dumplings are perfectly steamed.

Prawn biryani

 Hob   *Serves 4*

This might stretch the definition of biryani – but once you taste it you won't mind!

INGREDIENTS

- 2 tbsp oil
- 1 white onion, chopped
- 2 tbsp tikka masala curry paste
- 4 large tomatoes, chopped

- 400 g frozen king prawns
- 300 g basmati rice, washed
- 4 tbsp crispy onions
- 10 g coriander, leaves picked

METHOD

Warm oil in a large saucepan or casserole then add onion and a pinch of salt. Fry for 6–8 minutes, then add masala paste and tomatoes. Cook for 2–3 minutes. Add prawns and cook for 3–4 minutes. Add washed rice and stir. Add 600 ml boiling water and bring back to the boil. Cover and cook for 10 minutes, then remove from heat and leave to stand for 10 minutes. Rough up with a spoon and serve topped with crispy onions and coriander.

Pasta e fagioli

 Hob   *Serves 4*   (Vegan)

This dish turns a handful of simple ingredients into a meal more delicious than it has any right to be.

INGREDIENTS

4 tbsp olive oil

1 white onion, finely diced

2 sticks celery, finely diced

1 x 400-g tin plum tomatoes

2 x 400-g tins borlotti beans

200 g dried pasta

METHOD

Heat oil in a large pan over a medium heat. Add onion, celery and a pinch of salt and cook for 6–8 minutes until soft. Add tomatoes, bring to the boil and cook for 5 minutes. Then add the beans and their liquid, plus one tin of boiling water. Simmer for 10 minutes, or until the beans are tender. Add pasta, bring back to the boil and simmer for 8 minutes, adding more water if it seems too thick. Serve with a little extra olive oil.

Loaded mac and cheese

☐ *Oven*   ☐ *Air Fryer*   *Serves 4*

This no-holds-barred mac and cheese has everything you could possibly need in a meal – and more.

INGREDIENTS

2 tbsp olive oil

150 g bacon lardons

1 white onion, chopped

4 garlic cloves, grated

2 tbsp plain flour

1.5 litres whole milk

400 g macaroni pasta

200 g baby spinach or rocket, or a mixture

50 g sundried tomatoes, chopped

200 g mature cheddar cheese, grated

100 g panko breadcrumbs

50 g parmesan cheese, grated

METHOD

Preheat the oven to 200°C (air fryer; 175°C). In a wide shallow ovenproof or casserole pan, warm the oil over a medium heat. Add the lardons and cook for 3–5 minutes until they've released their fat and turned golden brown. Add the onion and garlic and a good pinch of salt. Cook for a further 6–8 minutes until soft and starting to brown. Add the flour and stir well, cooking out for 2–3 minutes so that you have a thick smooth paste. Add the milk, little by little, beating with a whisk so that you have a nice white sauce. Add the pasta, spinach, sundried tomatoes and cheddar, and stir to combine. Top with the breadcrumbs and parmesan and place in the hot oven for 15–20 minutes (air fryer; 12–15 minutes) until brown and bubbling on top. Allow to cool slightly before serving.

Cheat's chicken pie

🖾 *Oven*   🍳 *Air Fryer*   *Serves 4*

This recipe gives you a tasty pie in well under an hour.

INGREDIENTS

2 tbsp oil
1 leek, finely sliced
100 g button
   mushrooms, halved
400 g cooked chicken

250 g mascarpone
1 egg yolk
500 ml whole milk
8 sheets filo pastry

METHOD

Preheat oven to 200°C (air fryer; 175°C). In a wide, shallow ovenproof pan or casserole, warm oil over a medium heat. Add leek and a pinch of salt and cook for 6 minutes, stirring occasionally, then add mushrooms and cook for 4 minutes. Remove from the heat. Add chicken, mascarpone and egg yolk, mix well, then gradually add the milk, stirring until you have a loose sauce. Scrunch filo into loose balls and place on top. Drizzle with oil and bake for 20-25 minutes (air fryer; 16-20 minutes) until golden brown.

Speedy tartiflette

⊞ *Oven*　　🍶 *Air Fryer*　　　*Serves 4*

A traditional potato and cheese Alpine treat to keep the cold at bay.

INGREDIENTS

8 rashers of bacon, chopped

1 white onion, finely sliced

500 g new potatoes, sliced into rounds

2 tbsp olive oil

2 garlic cloves, grated

175 ml white wine

150 ml double cream

150 g Reblochon, or another melty cheese of your choice, diced

METHOD

Preheat oven to 200°C (air fryer; 175°C). Put bacon, onion, potatoes, oil, garlic and a pinch of salt into a medium-sized roasting tray. Roast for 20–25 minutes (air fryer; 15–20 minutes), until potato slices are just cooked. Remove from the oven. Add wine, cream and cheese and stir well. Return to the oven for 20 minutes (air fryer; 15 minutes), or until browning on top. Serve with a simple green salad.

Mighty green lasagne

☐ *Oven*   ☐ *Air Fryer*   *Serves 4*   (Vegetarian)

This is a light, bright take on a classic lasagne that works perfectly as a lunch or dinner throughout the year. By using fresh lasagne sheets this is ready in well under an hour, too.

INGREDIENTS

150 g goat's cheese, chopped

500 g ricotta

100 g vegetarian hard cheese

1 lemon, zested and juiced

4 tbsp olive oil

400 g frozen peas, defrosted

200 g baby spinach

300 g fresh lasagne sheets

10 g basil, torn

METHOD

Preheat the oven to 200°C (air fryer; 175°C). Start by mixing the goat's cheese, ricotta, 75 g of the vegetarian hard cheese, lemon zest and 2 tbsp of olive oil together in a bowl and seasoning with salt and pepper. Next, mix the defrosted peas and spinach together in a bowl, seasoning with lemon juice and the remaining oil.

To build the lasagne, place a layer of one third of the greens on the base of an ovenproof dish, dollop one quarter of the cheese mix onto this, then a layer of the fresh lasagne sheets. Repeat this three times before finishing with a layer of the cheese mix. Scatter the top layer with the remaining vegetarian hard cheese and a little drizzle of oil and place in the oven for 30–35 minutes (air fryer; 25–30 minutes) until the top layer is golden brown and melted. Allow to cool a little before serving topped with the torn basil.

Baked jollof-style rice

 Oven   *Air Fryer*   *Serves 4*   (*Vegan*)

A traditional West African accompaniment to a meal, or
the rich spicy rice can be enjoyed perfectly just as it is.

INGREDIENTS

3 red peppers, halved and deseeded

2 tbsp tomato purée

1 white onion, chopped

2 garlic cloves, grated

4 tsp fresh ginger, grated

1 Scotch bonnet chilli or 2–3 red chillies, seeds
and all, chopped

3 tbsp oil

1 tbsp dried thyme

2 tsp hot curry powder

400 g basmati rice, washed

100 g green beans, chopped into 2-cm pieces

METHOD

Heat the oven to 200°C (air fryer; 175°C). Put the peppers, tomato purée, onion, garlic, ginger and chilli in a food processor and blitz until a rough paste. Heat the oil in an ovenproof or casserole pan over medium heat. Add the blitzed pepper mixture and fry for 6–8 minutes, then add the thyme, curry powder and a good pinch of salt. Add the rice and fry together for 2 minutes before adding the green beans and 600 ml of boiling water. Bring everything to the boil, cover with a lid, place in the hot oven and bake for 25–30 minutes (air fryer; 20–25 minutes) until the rice is perfectly cooked.

Quick cassoulet

▦ *Oven*　　🍳 *Air Fryer*　　*Serves 4*

A classic French dish that brings together beans, pork, confit duck and sausage, baked in a pot called a cassoulet. Here we've cut a few corners and removed some of the excess fatty meat to give you an approximation of a cassoulet with little of the fuss.

INGREDIENTS

4 tbsp oil

1 white onion, finely chopped

2 sticks celery, finely chopped

2 medium carrots, finely chopped

4 garlic cloves, finely sliced

2 x 400-g tins cannellini beans, juice and all

1 x 400-g tins chopped tomatoes

2 bay leaves

200 g smoked sausage, such as frankfurter or kielbasa, cut into 1-cm rounds

200 g precooked chicken legs or drumsticks, whole

50 g dried breadcrumbs

METHOD

Preheat the oven to 200°C (air fryer; 175°C). Heat 3 tbsp oil in a large saucepan or casserole pan and sweat the onion, celery, carrots and garlic and a good pinch of salt for 6–8 minutes until softening. Add the cannellini beans, tomatoes and bay leaves and bring to a simmer before adding the smoked sausage and chicken. Remove from the heat and top with the breadcrumbs, drizzling the top with the remaining oil, before placing in the oven and cooking for 35–40 minutes (air fryer; approx. 30 minutes) until golden brown and delicious.

Deep-dish pizza pie

 Oven   *Serves 4*   (*Vegetarian*)

Deep-dish pizza may have lost fans to sourdough, but this recipe will have you fighting its corner once again.

INGREDIENTS

1 x 320-g ready-rolled
   shortcrust pastry

250 g grated
   mozzarella

1 x 400-g tin chopped
   tomatoes

250 g mozzarella balls,
   sliced into 0.5-mm
   rounds

1 tsp dried oregano

50 g grated vegetarian
   hard cheese

1 tbsp olive oil

10 g basil, leaves
   picked and torn

METHOD

Preheat oven to 180°C. Line a 20-cm pie dish with shortcrust pastry. Prick the base with a fork then lay down a third of the grated mozzarella. Spoon half of the tinned tomatoes over this, season with a pinch of salt, then top with half the sliced mozzarella. Repeat these layers. Top with oregano, hard cheese and oil and bake for 30 minutes. Allow to cool before serving and top with torn basil.

DINE IN STYLE

Sometimes you want to splash out and treat yourself or those you're cooking for. This need not be overly complicated – it might mean treating yourself to a special ingredient or spending the whole afternoon gently cooking a stew – but the result is a little more special because of it and everyone deserves to be spoiled sometimes.

Spanish chicken with chickpeas and peppers

🍳 *Oven*   🍟 *Air Fryer*   *Serves 4*

The sort of recipe that can transport you to a village square in rural Spain. It won't be long before this replaces the roast chicken you usually have for Sunday lunch.

INGREDIENTS

1 whole 1.5–2 kg chicken (chicken thighs will work too)

200 g cherry tomatoes

4 long red peppers, seeds removed and chopped into large pieces

1 x 400-g tin chickpeas, water and all

4 garlic cloves, halved

1 red onion, cut into eighths

2 tbsp red wine vinegar

2 tsp sweet smoked paprika

1 tsp hot smoked paprika (or cayenne pepper)

4 tbsp olive oil

½ lemon, juiced

METHOD

Preheat the oven to 200°C (air fryer; 175°C). Start by spatchcocking your chicken. Place the chicken breast-side down on a chopping board and using kitchen scissors to cut alongside the backbone on both sides to remove it. Flip the chicken over, splay out the legs and wings and press down hard on the breastbone so it is as flat as it will go. If you don't fancy spatchcocking, use chicken thighs instead.

In a high-sided baking tray large enough to hold the chicken, place the remaining ingredients, 2 tbsp oil and a pinch of salt. Place the chicken on top, breast-side up, drizzle with the remaining oil and season with salt. Place in the hot oven and cook for 45 minutes to 1 hour (air fryer; 40–50 minutes), or until the chicken is golden brown and cooked. Squeeze over the lemon juice, cut the chicken into chunks and serve on top of spoonfuls of the smoky, rich saucy chickpeas.

Sumac chicken wings with grape and pomegranate tabbouleh

 Oven   *Air Fryer*   *Serves 4*

Here the humble chicken wing is elevated to a decadent Middle Eastern-style show-stopper.

INGREDIENTS

800 g chicken wings

2 tsp ground cumin

2 tbsp sumac

1 tbsp dried chilli flakes

4 tbsp olive oil

1 red onion, sliced

400 g black grapes

200 g Tenderstem broccoli, whole

200 g bulgur wheat

80 g pomegranate seeds

50 g flat leaf parsley, finely chopped

1 lemon, juiced

METHOD

Preheat the oven to 200°C (air fryer; 175°C). Place the chicken wings in a high-sided roasting tray along with the cumin, sumac, chilli flakes, 2 tbsp oil and a pinch of salt. Mix well so that spices are spread evenly over each chicken wing. Distribute the onion, grapes and broccoli evenly and place the whole thing in the oven to cook for 35-40 minutes (air fryer; approx. 30 minutes). The wings should be starting to brown and the grapes should be bursting at the edges. Add the bulgur wheat to the pan, settling it in and around the wings, then pour over enough boiling water to cover the bulgur wheat. Cover the tray in tinfoil and return to the oven for 5 minutes (if using an air fryer, there is no need to cover the tray).

To serve, lift the wings out of the tray and place aside. Add the pomegranate seeds, parsley and lemon juice into the tray, mix well to fully combine, then serve topped with the chicken wings and a pinch or two of sumac.

Slow-cooked Korean short ribs and rice cakes

 Oven *Slow Cooker*   *Serves 4*

This dish couldn't be simpler to put together, but the key to its success is a very long, slow cook.

INGREDIENTS

1 bunch spring onions, roughly chopped

8 beef short ribs, approx. 6–8 cm long

4 tbsp oil

150 g Korean rice cakes (cylindrically shaped)

4 garlic cloves, sliced

1 stick fresh ginger, finely sliced

80 ml rice wine vinegar

75 g kimchi, chopped

2 tbsp light soy sauce

2 tbsp soft brown sugar

1 x 400-ml can lemonade (or from a bottle)

METHOD

Preheat the oven to 160°C. Set a small handful of spring onions, the short ribs, oil and rice cakes to one side. Place the rest of the ingredients in a blender and blitz to a smooth sauce. Heat the oil in a heavy-bottomed oven-proof saucepan or casserole pan over a high heat. Season the short ribs all over with some salt then brown them all over. Once browned, add the sauce to the pan, making sure it just covers the ribs (add a little more water if it doesn't). Bring to a simmer, cover the pan, then place in the oven for 3–4 hours, or until the bones slide out of the ribs without resistance. Check the braise sporadically, adding water if the pan starts to seem dry. Once cooked and completely soft, add the rice cakes (and a little more water if needed) and return to the oven for 15 minutes or until the rice cakes are soft. Sprinkle over the remaining spring onions to serve.

Hong Kong-style clay pot rice and tofu

 Hob　　 Slow Cooker　　Serves 4　　(Vegan)

This might sound abstemious to start with, but the rich tofu over delicious baked sticky rice is anything but. Try this once and it will become a go-to treat or a centrepiece for a dinner party, without doubt.

INGREDIENTS

2 tsp sesame oil

2 garlic cloves

2 tsp fresh ginger, grated

2 tbsp crispy chilli oil

2 tbsp light soy sauce

¼ tsp caster sugar

¼ tsp white pepper

1 small aubergine, cut into 2-cm cubes

1 x 300-g block firm tofu, cut into 2-cm cubes

180 g long-grain rice, washed

250 ml water

6 spring onions, finely chopped

METHOD

In a mixing bowl, combine the sesame oil, garlic, ginger, crispy chilli oil, soy sauce, sugar and pepper and whisk together. Add the aubergine and tofu to this mix and gently stir so everything is coated. Leave this to one side while you start your rice. Combine your washed rice with 250 ml water in a lidded saucepan and bring to a boil. Once boiling, place the aubergine and then tofu on top in as even a layer as possible and pour over the sauce. Cover the pot, turn the heat down to the lowest setting, and let everything simmer together for 10 minutes. Then take off the heat and leave to steam, lid still on, for 10 minutes. Finally, uncover the pan, add the spring onions, stir everything together, and check the seasoning, adding more soy sauce if necessary.

Thai prawn balls and coconut rice

 Hob   Slow Cooker   Serves 4

These fiery prawn balls are perfect against the richness of the coconut rice. That it's a case of bunging everything in a pot and letting time and patience do the work is all the better.

INGREDIENTS

500 g raw king prawns, shells removed

2 garlic cloves, grated

2 tsp fresh ginger, grated

2 Thai bird's eye chillies

4 tsp light soy sauce

3 tsp fish sauce

2 shallots, finely chopped

2 tbsp Thai red curry paste

400 g long-grain rice, washed

1 x 400-ml tin coconut milk

200 g green beans, top and tailed and cut in half

25 g Thai basil (or mint, torn)

METHOD

In a blender, combine the raw prawns, garlic, ginger, chillies, 2 tsp soy sauce and 1 tsp fish sauce. Blitz to a paste then use wet hands to form into golf ball-sized balls. In a small bowl, whisk together 2 tsp soy sauce, 2 tsp fish sauce, the shallots and the red curry paste. Add the washed rice, coconut milk and 200 ml boiling water to a lidded saucepan and bring to the boil. Add the green beans and prawn balls on top of the rice and pour over the sauce. Cover the pot, turn the heat down to the lowest setting, and let everything simmer together for 10 minutes. Then take off the heat and leave to steam, not removing the lid for 10 minutes. Finally, uncover the pan, add the herbs, stir everything together and check the seasoning, adding more soy sauce if necessary.

Mackerel with chorizo, peppers and potato

 Oven  Air Fryer   Serves 4

Often this is made with white fish, such as cod, but somehow the oily mackerel over the smoky rich peppers and potatoes makes this more decadent and feel like a real treat.

INGREDIENTS

400 g waxy potatoes, peeled and cut into 3-cm pieces

2 long red peppers, seeds removed, finely sliced

200 g soft cooking chorizo, sliced

1 red onion, finely sliced

4 garlic cloves, finely sliced

200 ml white wine

4 tbsp olive oil

8 mackerel fillets (or 4 whole mackerel, filleted)

1 tbsp sherry vinegar

25 g flat leaf parsley, leaves picked and chopped

METHOD

Preheat the oven to 200°C (air fryer; 175°C). Combine the potato, peppers, chorizo, onion, garlic, white wine, 2 tbsp oil and a good pinch of salt in a large roasting tray and mix well. Cover with tinfoil and place in the hot oven for 35-40 minutes (air fryer; 25-30 minutes) until the potatoes are cooked through. Remove the tinfoil and lay the mackerel fillets on top, skin-side up, seasoning them with a little salt and the remaining oil. Place this back in the oven for 8-10 minutes (air fryer; approx. 5 minutes) or until the mackerel is flaky and cooked. Remove the mackerel and season the potato mixture with the sherry vinegar and more salt if needed before stirring through the parsley and serving alongside the mackerel.

Duck and lentils

 Oven   *Serves 4*

If you want to feel sophisticated and mildly French for an evening, then this is the dish for you.

INGREDIENTS

2 tbsp olive oil

1 white onion, finely diced

2 sticks celery, finely diced

10 sundried tomatoes, chopped

2 garlic cloves, grated

1 x 400-g tin green or puy lentils

175 ml white wine

2 tbsp red wine vinegar

1 tbsp Dijon mustard

200 g greens such as cavolo nero, kale or spinach

4 duck legs (from a tin is fine)

METHOD

Preheat the oven to 200°C. Combine everything in a large high-sided roasting tray, adding all the liquid from the lentils plus one more tin of boiling water. Pop the duck legs on top of the lentils, trying to make sure they don't sink down, then tightly cover the tray with tinfoil. Place this in the oven for an hour. After an hour, check that the duck legs are cooked and the lentils haven't dried out, adding more water if they have, and return to the oven uncovered for a final 10 minutes to crisp up the duck skin. Allow to cool slightly before serving.

Hainanese chicken and rice

 Hob　　 *Slow Cooker*　　　*Serves 4*

This is a joyously simple Chinese dish that will find you boiling a whole chicken filled with rice, which is fun, delicious and an impressive thing to serve if you have friends over.

INGREDIENTS

1 whole 1.5–2-kg chicken

250 g jasmine rice, washed

8 spring onions

1 stick fresh ginger; 4 cm sliced into rounds, 2 cm grated

5 garlic cloves; 3 halved, 2 grated

2 tbsp light soy sauce

1 tbsp sesame oil

2 tbsp oil

2 tbsp crispy chilli oil

METHOD

Season the cavity of your chicken with salt then pour the rice into the cavity. Using a toothpick or skewer, secure the cavity of the chicken so that the rice stays inside. Place this in a large pan and cover with water. Add the spring onions, the rounds of ginger, the halved garlic cloves, soy sauce and sesame oil. Place over a high heat and bring to a boil. Boil for 5 minutes, then pop on a lid and remove from the heat. Leave to stand for 60 minutes. Meanwhile, combine the ginger, grated garlic, oil and a pinch of salt and mix well. To serve, remove the chicken and scoop the cooked rice out of the cavity. Dress the rice with the ginger and garlic sauce. Portion the chicken. Divide the rice and chicken between bowls, then ladle in some of the broth and top with crispy chilli oil.

Pot roast beef and celeriac

 Oven   *Serves 4*

This is a hearty winter warmer that can go into the oven and be forgotten about for hours.

INGREDIENTS

2 tbsp oil
1 kg topside of beef, whole
1 tbsp plain flour
2 leeks, cut into 4-cm pieces
4 sticks celery, cut into 2-cm pieces
2 large carrots, cut into 4-cm pieces
500 g celeriac, peeled and cut into chunks
6 garlic cloves, finely sliced
2 bay leaves
200 ml red wine
1 x 400-g tin chopped tomatoes

METHOD

Preheat the oven to 160°C. Heat the oil in a large saucepan or casserole pan over a high heat. Season the beef all over with salt and pepper then dust with the flour. Brown this on all sides in the pan then remove to one side. Add the leeks, celery, carrots and celeriac to the pan, and cook for a couple of minutes. Add the garlic, cook for 30 seconds, then add the wine, making sure to scrape all the nice dark, sticky bits from the base of the pan. Add the tinned tomatoes and bay leaves, then place the beef back into the pan, topping up with boiling water so the beef and veg are almost covered. Put the lid on the pan and place in the oven for at least 2 hours, or until the beef pulls apart with very little encouragement. To serve, portion the beef and vegetables and serve with some fresh crusty bread and butter.

Mushroom moussaka

 Oven *Serves 4* (*Vegan*)

Here we're using mushrooms and lentils to turn this into a seriously decadent vegan treat.

INGREDIENTS

1 large aubergine, cut into 1-cm rounds

4 tbsp olive oil

1 red onion, finely sliced

2 garlic cloves, grated

350 g chestnut mushrooms, chopped or blitzed into tiny pieces

1 x 400-g tin lentils

400 g tomato passata

1 tbsp dried oregano

10 g mint, leaves picked and chopped

500 g waxy potatoes, peeled and sliced into 0.5-cm rounds

200 g vegan cream cheese

METHOD

Lightly salt the aubergine slices on both sides and leave to one side for an hour.

Heat 1 tbsp oil in a casserole over a medium heat and fry the aubergine for a few minutes on each side until browned and crispy. Set to one side to cool.

Preheat the oven to 200°C. Heat the remaining 3 tbsp oil in the same pan or casserole over a medium heat and sweat the onion and garlic with a pinch of salt for 6-8 minutes until soft. Add the mushrooms and cook for 6-8 minutes until browned, then add the lentils, juice and all, passata and oregano. Bring to the boil and simmer for 10-15 minutes, add the mint and leave to one side. Finally, layer the aubergine over the tomatoey mushrooms, then add a layer of sliced potatoes, repeating until all have been used up. Carefully spread the top layer with the cream cheese and drizzle with a little more oil. Place in the oven and cook for 45 minutes until the top is bubbling and golden and the potatoes are cooked. Serve with green salad.

Coq au vin

 Hob   *Serves 4*

This French classic ticks all the boxes for a decadent one-pan supper that is equal parts showstopping and cosy.

INGREDIENTS

50 g butter

2 tbsp olive oil

1.8 kg chicken pieces, skin on

150 g lardons or smoked bacon cut into 1-cm strips

150 g whole button mushrooms

100 g pickled silverskin onions

4 garlic cloves, finely sliced

2 tbsp plain flour

150 g baby new potatoes, halved

100 g peas, fresh or frozen

250 ml red wine

2 bay leaves

METHOD

In a large pan over a high heat, melt the butter and oil together. Season the chicken pieces with salt and pepper and brown in the hot pan skin-side down. Leave the chicken to one side while you cook off the bacon until golden brown then add the mushrooms, pickled onions and garlic, browning these in the hot bacony oil. Add the flour and stir well to coat everything, then cook for 2–3 minutes. Finally, add the potatoes and peas, season again with a pinch of salt before adding the wine, bay leaves and enough boiling water to just cover the vegetables. Place the chicken pieces on top, cover and reduce to a simmer, allowing to gently bubble for 20–30 minutes until the chicken and potatoes are cooked. Serve as it is, or with some bread to mop up all the tasty sauce.

Reimagined jambalaya

 Oven   *Air Fryer*   *Serves 4*   (Vegan)

Transport yourself to New Orleans with this twist on a classic that will have you and your taste buds dancing in jubilation.

INGREDIENTS

4 tbsp olive oil

1 white onion, diced

2 sticks celery, diced

2 carrots, diced

1 red pepper, chopped

4 garlic cloves, finely sliced

2 tsp sweet smoked paprika

½ tsp cayenne pepper

2 tsp dried oregano

250 g long-grain rice

1 x 400-g tin chopped tomatoes

200 g frozen okra (or peas/sweetcorn/ green beans if you can't find okra)

1 x 400-g tin black-eyed peas or black beans

2 tsp Tabasco

½ lemon, juiced

25 g flat leaf parsley, chopped

METHOD

Heat the oven to 200°C (air fryer; 175°C). Heat the oil in a heavy-based or casserole pan over a medium heat. Add the onion, celery, carrot, pepper and a good pinch of salt and cook for 8-10 minutes until soft and just starting to colour. Add the garlic, paprika, cayenne and dried oregano and cook for a further minute, before adding the rice and cooking together for another minute or so. Finally, add the tinned tomatoes and 500 ml of boiling water. Bring to the boil, then cover with a lid and place in the oven for 20 minutes (air fryer; 16 minutes). Remove from the oven, add the okra and beans to the pan and stir through, before putting the lid back on and finishing in the oven for a further 10 minutes (air fryer; 8 minutes). To serve, add the Tabasco, lemon juice and parsley and stir to combine.

Smoky chipotle turkey crispy tacos

 Hob   Slow Cooker   Serves 4

This might raise some eyebrows due to the dark chocolate used to give the sauce its distinctive depth of flavour, but don't let that put you off – this is a crowd-pleaser like no other.

INGREDIENTS

600 g turkey mince (or pork/chicken/vegetarian mince if you prefer)

2 tsp cumin

1 tsp chipotle chilli flakes

2 tbsp oil

1 red onion, chopped

4 tsp fresh ginger, grated

6 garlic cloves, finely grated

50 g dark chocolate, finely grated

1 x 400-g tin chopped tomatoes

2 tbsp red wine vinegar

1 lime, juiced

8 hard-shell tacos

100 g sour cream

**75 g mild cheddar,
grated**

**50 g coriander, leaves
picked and chopped**

METHOD

Season the mince with cumin, chilli flakes and a good
pinch of salt. Heat the oil in a shallow pan over a
medium heat and fry the seasoned mince until browned
all over. Add the onions, ginger and garlic and cook for
8-10 minutes, stirring occasionally. Then add the dark
chocolate, tomatoes, vinegar, one tomato tin full of
boiling water and bring to a simmer. Turn the heat to low
and cook for 45-50 minutes until you have a dark, thick
mince. Check on it occasionally as it's cooking, adding
a little hot water if needed. Season with lime juice and
more salt if you desire. To serve, fill the hard-shell tacos
with the mince and top each one with sour cream, cheese
and coriander.

Cotriade

 Hob   *Serves 4*

This French fish and vegetable stew is traditionally served spooned over slightly stale bread, which sounds odd, but is a real treat worth trying.

INGREDIENTS

2 tbsp olive oil

1 white onion, sliced

1 head fennel, sliced

2 garlic cloves, finely sliced

12–15 strands saffron

450 g waxy potatoes, peeled and cut into 3-cm pieces

150 g broad beans or peas

175 ml white wine

4 large tomatoes, chopped

600 ml fish stock

750 g cod, hake or haddock fillets, fresh

½ lemon, juiced

METHOD

Heat the oil in a large saucepan or casserole pan over a medium heat and sweat the onion, fennel and a good pinch of salt for 8 minutes, stirring regularly. Add the garlic and saffron and cook for a further 2 minutes. Add the potatoes, broad beans and another pinch of salt and cover the pan with a lid, cooking for 8–10 minutes until the potatoes are almost cooked through. Add the wine, letting it spit and simmer for a few minutes, before adding the tomatoes and fish stock and bringing back to the boil. Add the fish fillets on top of the vegetables, pop the lid on again and cook for a final 6–8 minutes until the fish is perfectly flaky and cooked. Season with the lemon juice and serve. You can eat this just as it is, but why not try it spooned over stale bread?

Drunken Irish mussels

 Hob   *Serves 4*

To call these drunken is not to cast aspersions, but simmering away in cider is certain to leave its mark on anyone.

INGREDIENTS

50 g butter

2 shallots, finely chopped

2 sticks celery, finely chopped

1 leek, finely chopped

400 g waxy potatoes, peeled and cut into 1-cm cubes

2 kg fresh mussels

600 ml cider

10 g flat leaf parsley, chopped

½ lemon, juiced

100 ml single cream

METHOD

Heat the butter over a medium-low heat in a saucepan large enough to accommodate all the mussels. Sweat the shallots, celery and leek with a good pinch of salt for 8–10 minutes, stirring occasionally, until completely soft. Add the potato and another pinch of salt, cooking for 5–6 minutes until also soft. Add the mussels and increase the heat to high. Stir well so the potato mixture combines completely with the mussels, then add the cider and immediately cover with a tight-fitting lid. Cook for 6–8 minutes until the mussels are all open, discarding any that aren't, then remove from the heat and add the parsley, lemon juice and cream. Divide between bowls and serve with crusty bread to mop up all the delicious sauce.

Potato, cheese and onion pie

 Oven   *Serves 4*   (*Vegetarian*)

It is a kind of magic to witness the alchemy of three humble ingredients becoming something with such depth and complexity once wrapped in pastry and baked.

INGREDIENTS

2 packs ready-rolled shortcrust pastry

125 g salted butter

4 white onions, finely sliced

4 large waxy potatoes (about 0.8–1 kg), very finely sliced

100 g Lancashire cheese (or any sharp hard cheese), grated

10 ml milk

METHOD

Line a springform cake tin with one roll of pastry, leaving a little overhang. Place in the fridge. Melt the butter in a saucepan over medium heat, adding the onions and a pinch of salt. Reduce the heat to low and cook in the foaming butter, stirring regularly, for 40 minutes until the onions are soft, brown and sweet. While the onions are cooking, soak your sliced potato in cold water and preheat the oven to 160°C. Spread a thin layer of the cooked onions on the base of your lined tin, then layer potato slices in a single overlapping layer and sprinkle over cheese. Repeat until all the filling is in the pie. Once the pie is filled, top with remaining pastry and press the edges together. Brush the pie top with milk, cut a little cross in the middle and place in the oven to cook for 1–1.5 hours. When ready, the pie should look golden brown and a skewer placed into the centre should pass through without any resistance. Serve with English mustard and a fresh salad.

Seafood risotto

 Hob   *Serves 4*

This is a truly luxurious risotto that is likely a once-in-a-blue-moon treat.

INGREDIENTS

750 ml fish stock

50 g unsalted butter

2 tbsp oil

1 white onion, finely diced

2 sticks celery, finely diced

250 g risotto rice

100 ml white wine

12 strands fresh saffron

8 scallops, cut into 2-cm pieces

8 king prawns, peeled and cut into 2-cm pieces

50 g parmesan, grated

10 g flat leaf parsley, finely chopped

METHOD

Boil just over 750 ml of water in the kettle, replace into a jug, whisk in the fish stock cubes and leave to one side. Heat half the butter and all of the oil in a wide shallow pan over a medium-low heat, and sweat the onion and celery with a pinch of salt for 10–12 minutes until soft but not coloured. Increase the heat to medium-high and add the rice. Cook for 2 minutes, stirring all the time, then add the white wine and reduce. Add the saffron and two ladles of stock, bringing to a simmer then reducing the heat to low. Cook, stirring almost constantly, for 20 minutes, continuing to add more stock whenever the pan starts to dry out. Check the rice and, once cooked, add the seafood, stir and remove from the heat and cover. Let the residual heat in the pan lightly cook the scallops and prawns for 5–6 minutes. Finally, add the remaining butter and the parmesan to the pan and stir well. Scatter with the parsley and serve with a lemon wedge.

Prawn and 'nduja lasagne

⬛ *Oven*　　🍳 *Air Fryer*　　　*Serves 4*

This is very much a luxurious take on an old favourite.
The combination of hot and spicy 'nduja and the sweet
prawns is unexpectedly delicious. Once you've tried this it
will be hard to go back.

INGREDIENTS

200 g baby spinach

400 g ricotta

1 egg yolk

125 g parmesan, grated

1 lemon, zested and juiced

400 g king prawns, peeled and roughly chopped

150 g fresh 'nduja (or chorizo if 'nduja is hard
　to find)

600 ml tomato passata

12 fresh lasagne sheets

2 large balls of mozzarella, finely sliced

METHOD

Preheat oven to 200°C (air fryer; 175°C). Start by mixing the spinach, ricotta, egg yolk, a pinch of salt, 50 g grated parmesan and the lemon zest in a bowl and mix well using your hands, scrunching the spinach to create a sauce consistency as you go. Similarly, combine the prawns, 'nduja, lemon juice and 4 tbsp passata in a separate bowl and mix well. Finally, spread a quarter of the ricotta mix over the base of a rectangular baking dish. Top this with a quarter of the prawn mix, a quarter of the remaining passata and four lasagne sheets. Repeat this for the remaining ingredients. Cover the top layer of the lasagne with sliced mozzarella and the remaining parmesan. Place in the oven and cook for 35–40 minutes (air fryer; 30–35 minutes) until golden and bubbling on top. Leave to cool slightly before serving as is or with a green salad.

Recipe index

THE LITTLE BOOK OF
VEGAN STUDENT FOOD

Jai Breitnauer

Paperback
ISBN: 978-1-83799-276-8

A pocket-sized guide to all things vegan grub, this little book is the perfect gift for students. Featuring an array of budget-friendly, flavourful and easy-to-make meals, this book gives you the vegan recipes you need to spice up your student suppers.

THE LITTLE BOOK OF
CURRY

Rufus Cavendish

Paperback
ISBN: 978-1-80007-417-0

From rogan josh and rendang to bunny chow and vindaloo, dive into this celebration of one of the world's most popular dishes: curry. Including the history of curry around the world, tips on growing your own spices, delicious recipes you can cook yourself and much more, *The Little Book of Curry* will help you spice up your life one dish at a time.

Have you enjoyed this book?
If so, find us on Facebook at **SUMMERSDALE PUBLISHERS**,
on Twitter/X at **@SUMMERSDALE** and on Instagram and
TikTok at **@SUMMERSDALEBOOKS** and get in touch.
We'd love to hear from you!

WWW.SUMMERSDALE.COM